MAR -- 2019

DATE DUE

Meet NASA Inventor Kendra Short and Her

Printable Probes
and
Cosmic Confetti

WORLD
BOOK

www.worldbook.com

World Book, Inc.
180 North LaSalle Street
Suite 900
Chicago, Illinois 60601
USA

For information about other World Book publications, visit our website at www.worldbook.com or call 1-800-WORLDBK (967-5325).

For information about sales to schools and libraries, call 1-800-975-3250 (United States), or 1-800-837-5365 (Canada).

Library of Congress Cataloging-in-Publication Data for this volume has been applied for.

Out of This World
978-0-7166-6155-9 (set, hc.)

Printable Probes and Cosmic Confetti
ISBN: 978-0-7166-6158-0 (hc.)

Also available as:
ISBN: 978-0-7166-6167-2 (e-book)

Printed in China by Shenzhen Donnelley Printing Co., Ltd., Guangdong Province
1st printing June 2017

Staff

Contents

Glossary There is a glossary of terms on page 45. Terms defined in the glossary are in boldface type that **looks like this** on their first appearance on any spread (two facing pages).

Pronunciations (how to say words) are given in parentheses the first time some difficult words appear in the book. They look like this: pronunciation (pruh NUHN see AY shuhn).

Introduction

Sending a space **probe** to Mars is a difficult task. The planet lies millions of miles or kilometers from Earth, so to get there in a reasonable time, the probe must travel at astonishing speeds. Once it reaches the Red Planet, the probe must slow itself with rockets to avoid just whizzing by. Slowing the craft enables it to take up **orbit** around Mars.

If the craft is a **lander,** it must then lower itself from orbit to the Martian surface. The gravitational pull at the surface of Mars is only about one-third that on Earth. But that is still strong enough to make for a bumpy landing. Previous landers have used rockets and parachutes to break their fall. Some have even used airbags to cushion their bounce on the rocky surface. All of these systems must be carefully engineered to prevent damage to the lander's scientific equipment.

Mechanical engineer Kendra Short was thinking about these problems when she came up with an unusual solution. Landers are bulky, expensive, and relatively fragile. Short tried to imagine a different kind of lander, one that could be simply dropped from the Martian sky, without the need for complicated landing systems.

Imagine dropping a traditional lander from the top of a tall building. Even the hardiest craft would shatter to pieces on the sidewalk below. Now imagine dropping a sheet of paper from the same height. The paper might float and flutter for some distance, but there is a good chance it would arrive on the ground unharmed.

A landing craft falls into the atmosphere of Mars packed inside a protective covering called an **aeroshell**.

Unlike a traditional space **probe,** paper is lightweight and flexible. Short is working to develop paper-like spacecraft that share these qualities. And while most probes are carefully crafted by hand, Short's probes are designed to be printed using a device not so different from an ordinary computer printer. Cheap and easy to make, flexible and lightweight, such probes could one day rain down like cosmic confetti on the Martian surface, gathering huge amounts of information about conditions on the Red Planet.

Meet Kendra Short.

❚❚ I'm a **mechanical engineer** at NASA's Jet Propulsion Laboratory in Pasadena, California. As a child, I dreamed of becoming an astronaut. Now I'm working to develop printable spacecraft that will help us explore the solar system. ❚❚

The NASA Innovative Advanced Concepts program. The titles in the *Out of This World* series feature projects that have won grant money from a group formed by the United States National Aeronautics and Space Administration, or NASA. The NASA Innovative Advanced Concepts program (NIAC) provides funding to teams working to develop bold new advances in space technology. You can visit NIAC's website at www.nasa.gov/niac.

Destination: Mars

Mars is the fourth planet from the sun and one of Earth's nearest neighbors. Ancient people named Mars after the Roman god of war because of the planet's reddish color. Scientists now know that the rusty hue comes from *iron oxide* (a combination of the elements iron and oxygen) in the rock and dust that cover the Martian surface. On Earth, this is the same compound that makes up rust.

Of all the bodies in the solar system, Mars has the surface that most looks like that of Earth. Mars has plains, canyons, mountains, volcanoes, ice caps, and even dust storms.

Since telescopes first revealed such Earthlike features, people have thought a lot about the idea of Martian life. But the surface of Mars appears to have no living things on it.

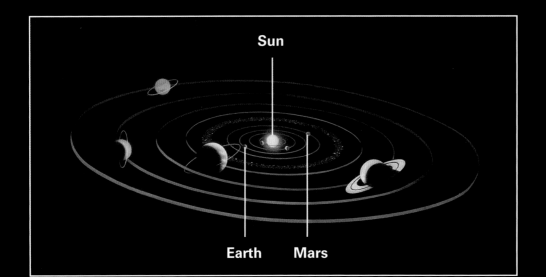

Sun

Earth   Mars

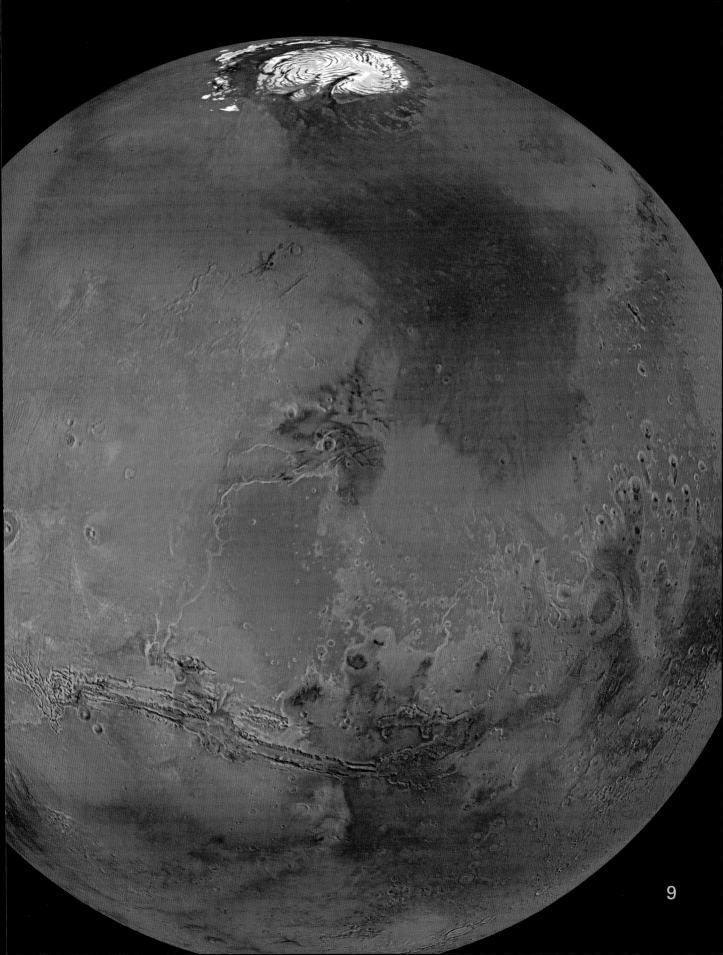

9

There are a few major differences between Earth and Mars that make the Red Planet a harsher place to live. Although Mars is the very next planet out from the sun, it is about half again as far from the sun as is Earth. So Mars receives less sunlight, helping to make the planet pretty chilly. Temperatures on the Martian surface average a frosty -80 °F (-60 °C).

Also, Mars has only $\frac{1}{10}$ Earth's mass. (Mass is the amount of stuff, or matter, that a thing is made of.) With less mass, there is less gravity on Mars to hold things close to it. So over time most of the atmosphere of Mars has floated away into space. Today, atmospheric pressure at the Martian surface is about $\frac{1}{100}$ that on Earth. Under such low pressures, any liquid water on the Martian surface would quickly boil away, even at cold temperatures. Scientists consider water to be a key ingredient in the development of life.

Still, scientists have reason to be hopeful of finding life on Mars. They have identified strong evidence that salty liquid water exists just beneath the Martian surface. Further evidence suggests that large amounts of water flowed over the planet's surface in the distant past. At such times, Mars may have been much more likely to harbor life than it is today. If life developed on Mars, some of it may have survived underground as surface conditions grew harsh.

Scientists have another reason to be interested in the Red Planet— it is a likely target for human space exploration. Placing astronauts on Mars would be challenging, but it is a major priority for the world's space programs.

Wind and ancient water are thought to have shaped these Martian surface features. A thin layer of water frost appears on the Martian surface (bottom right).

Follow the water

On Earth, life is found just about everywhere we look. Hardy living things survive in the bitter chill of Antarctica, in the heat of underwater volcanic vents, and at the heights of Earth's atmosphere. But everywhere life is found it requires some kind of water. So, in searching for life beyond Earth, scientists look for places in the solar system where liquid water is likely to be found. Mars is one of those places.

Exploring the Red Planet

Over the years, people have launched more than 50 missions to Mars. In 1964, the United States **probe** Mariner 4 became the first spacecraft to complete a successful flyby of the planet. It was followed in 1969 by Mariners 6 and 7. By chance, the three craft viewed only heavily cratered regions of the planet as they zipped past, sending back images of a lifeless, moonlike surface.

Our view of Mars changed dramatically in 1971 when the Mariner 9 probe **orbited** the planet, mapping 80 percent of its surface. This craft produced the first images of Mars's volcanoes and canyons. It also revealed features that appeared to have been carved by water, such as outflow channels and valley networks.

The United States Viking mission, launched in 1975, greatly expanded our knowledge of the Red Planet. Viking included two **orbiters** and two **landers,** which successfully lowered themselves to the surface in 1976. The landers took close-up pictures of the Martian surface and analyzed the soil, finding no strong evidence of life.

The first color image of Mars taken by the Viking 1 lander.

13

Since the mid-1990's, many **orbiters** have been sent to Mars. These **probes** have carried a wide range of scientific instruments able to study the Martian world. Together, they have helped scientists to develop a detailed understanding of the whole planet.

Surface exploration started again in 1995 with the launch of the United States Mars Pathfinder mission. The Pathfinder lander carried a small **rover** called Sojourner, not much bigger than a skateboard. The rover rolled a little over 300 feet (100 meters) in total, visiting several Martian rocks.

The two U.S. Mars Exploration Rovers landed on the planet in 2004. These golf cart-sized rovers became among the most successful probes in the history of space exploration. They were initially meant to operate for only 90 days. But one rover, nicknamed Spirit, continued to explore the planet for five years. The other, Opportunity, lasted even longer. By 2016, Opportunity had traveled over 26 miles (43 kilometers) on its Martian marathon. The two craft sent back detailed images of the planet's ground features. They provided the first certain evidence that liquid water once covered large areas of the planet's surface.

An even bigger rover, the United States Mars Science Laboratory, landed on the planet in 2012. The rover, nicknamed Curiosity, continued the work of the robotic geologists Spirit and Opportunity, analyzing Martian rocks and soil for clues to the planet's past.

The rover Curiosity took this self-portrait on the Martian surface in 2015.

Inventor feature:
Dreams of spaceflight

As a child, Kendra Short was interested in science and mathematics. When she was in third grade, her father took her to a telescope outing hosted by a local astronomy club.

❚❚ I remember looking through a telescope and seeing the rings of the planet Saturn. It was the most amazing thing I had ever seen. I thought, 'Gosh, you can actually see something that far away! What else is out there?' ❚❚ —Kendra

Short dreamed of becoming an astronaut and of visiting places like those she had seen through the telescope. She was an avid reader, taking in every bit of information she could get her hands on. She was lucky enough to live in the San Francisco Bay area, not too far from NASA's Ames Research Center in Mountain View, California. In high school, her guidance counselor helped her get a summer job there through NASA's Summer High

School Apprenticeship Research Program (SHARP).

" Ames does a lot of life science research, so I got to work with rhesus monkeys doing zero-gravity simulations. It was a tremendous summer. It locked things in for me, as far as what I wanted to do with my life. **"** —Kendra

Short studied engineering in college, earning a bachelor's degree from Princeton University and a master's degree from Stanford University. Afterward, she went to work for NASA's Jet Propulsion Laboratory (JPL), a center for the design and control of robotic spacecraft.

" I did apply to become an astronaut. I still had not given up on that dream. I think there is some part of a person that remains a third-grader forever. **"** —Kendra

It is difficult to get the job of an astronaut. Only a handful of candidates are selected from thousands of applications. Short was not one of them.

" By then, I really enjoyed what I was doing at JPL. I was able to explore space through the use of robotic spacecraft. I figured that if I never got out there myself, I was okay with that. **"** —Kendra

Failing (and succeeding) on Mars

Despite the many successes, exploring Mars is tricky business. Nearly two-thirds of missions sent to Mars have failed. Many of the missions failed on the launching pad. Others did not make it to Mars or were lost to communication once they arrived there.

Landing on Mars is particularly difficult. The Martian atmosphere is too thin to land a craft using parachutes alone. Mars missions typically employ a combination of parachutes, **retrorockets** (rockets used for braking), and other technologies to slow a **lander's** descent and ease it onto the ground.

In 1973, the Soviet Union (a country that existed from 1922 until 1991) launched two Mars missions involving landers. The lander of the Mars 6 mission is thought to have crashed into the planet when its retrorockets failed to fire. Retrorockets also malfunctioned on the Mars 7 mission, leading the craft to speed by the planet, missing it entirely.

The British lander Beagle 2 appears in an artist's conception (inset). The failed craft and parts of its landing equipment were later identified in an image produced by the United States Mars Reconnaissance Orbiter.

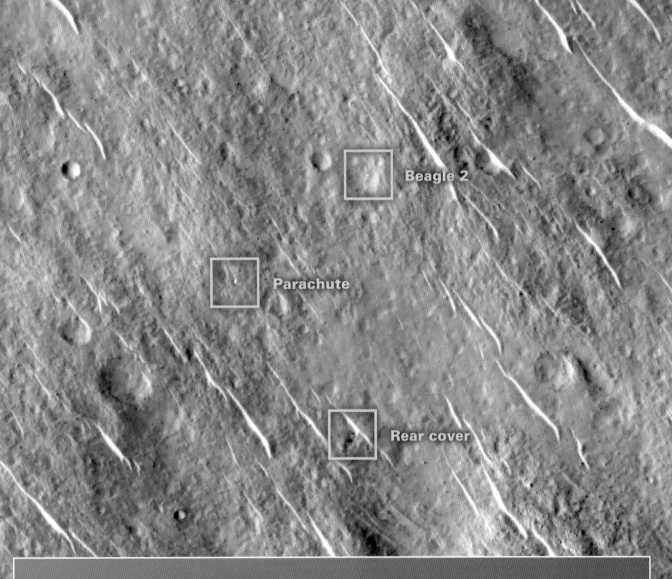

Beagle 2

Parachute

Rear cover

Two Soviet missions also attempted landings on Mars's moon Phobos. Mission controllers lost contact with the Phobos 1 craft in 1988, somewhere between Earth and Mars. The Phobos 2 craft lost contact in 1989, just before it was supposed to release two landers.

United States failures include the Mars Polar Lander, launched in 1999. The craft is thought to have crashed into the planet when mission managers shut off its engines too soon.

The landing successes of the early 2000's were made possible by a complex combination of technologies. The Mars Exploration Rovers made use of parachutes and **retrorockets** to halt their descent meters above the ground. The craft then deployed, or put out, airbags to cushion their final drop, bouncing to rest on the Martian surface. The Mars Science Laboratory went one step farther. It was delivered to the service by a hovering "sky crane," a hovering platform that lowered the **rover** on a tether.

The sophisticated systems of the early 2000's sometimes failed, too. The British lander Beagle 2 was lost after being deployed by the European Space Agency's Mars Express mission in 2003. The craft landed safely but failed to deploy all its solar panels, preventing it from communicating with mission controllers.

In this artist's conception, a hovering "sky crane" uses a tether to lower the Mars Science Laboratory to the Martian surface.

A more flexible approach

One day in the early 2000's, Kendra Short found herself considering the difficulties of landing such complicated Mars missions.

" These craft are always big and heavy, and they cost a lot of money. I was manager of the mechanical systems division at JPL, and we were responsible for delivering these **landers** safely to the surface. It was our job to design all the **aeroshells** [coverings that protect craft as they enter the atmosphere] and the parachutes and the airbags. **"** —Kendra

Short was talking in her office with a colleague, the astronomer and engineer David Van Buren. Van Buren was working on a different problem, one requiring spacecraft that could change their shape in space.

" In our brainstorming, we both started converging on a common solution: **flexible printed electronics. "** —Kendra

Both engineers had heard of advances in electronics that could be printed on thin, flexible sheets of plastic. The result was an electronic component that could bend and flex without breaking. For Van Buren, the flexibility of such electronics made them a promising material for use in shape-changing spacecraft. Short began to envision a network of lightweight, paperlike landers that could flutter to the Martian surface like confetti.

"It was in a moment of frustration that I thought, 'It takes so much to get these rovers to the surface. Can't we just throw them out of the aeroshell and let them land?' " —Kendra

What is a circuit?

At its heart, every robotic spacecraft is a piece of electronic equipment, something like a television or a computer. Electronic devices are made up of **circuits.** A circuit can be thought of as a tiny track or maze for carrying electric charges.

As electric charges zip around a circuit, they carry information in the form of **electric signals.** A circuit consists of pathways and switches designed to carry and manipulate, or handle, electric signals. Depending on its layout, a circuit may control, modify (change), amplify (make bigger or stronger), or process such signals.

Robotic spacecraft use circuits to gather data from their instruments. They also use circuits to process this data and to transmit the data back to Earth. Other circuits help to control any moving parts on the spacecraft.

There are two types of circuits commonly used in electronics. A **conventional circuit** is made up of stripes of conductive material printed on a flat piece of material, often a rigid plastic board. In an **integrated circuit,** the pathways and switches are etched into a type of material called a semiconductor. The semiconductor is usually a chip of silicon. Integrated circuits are generally what we think of when we think of computer chips.

Conventional circuits are cheaper to manufacture than are integrated circuits. But integrated circuits tend to be smaller, faster, and better at processing electric signals. Most electronic devices consist of a combination of conventional and integrated circuits.

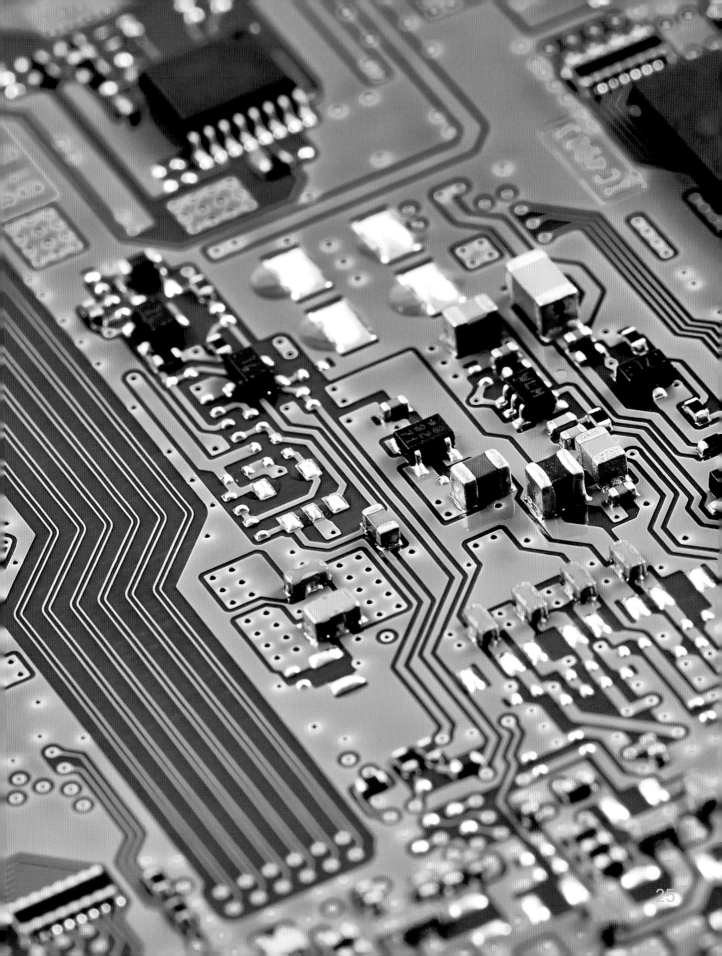

Big idea:
flexible electronics

Both **conventional circuits** and **integrated circuits** tend to be rigid, or stiff.

❚❚ But if you were to open up a home electronic device, such as a DVR or cell phone, you might notice some circuits printed on flexible material. ❚❚ —Kendra

Flexible printed electronics, much like conventional electronics, consist of pathways of conductive material bonded to a flat piece of material. But in flexible printed electronics, the material is a thin sheet of flexible plastic, rather than a rigid plastic board. The pathways themselves are printed using a flexible, conductive "ink." The result is a **circuit** that can flex and bend without breaking.

Simple flexible circuits have been in use for years. But advances in materials science and printing technology are greatly expanding the capabilities of flexible printed electronics.

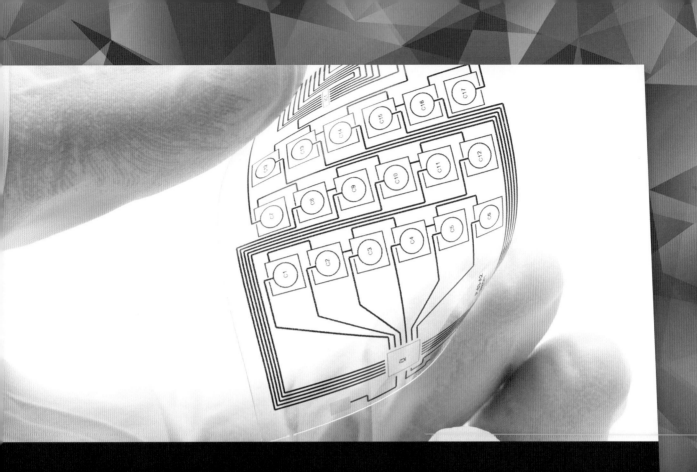

One example is a simple light **sensor.** It can be created by printing a layer of light-sensitive "ink" onto flexible plastic. Light falling on the light-sensitive material can change its ability to conduct electric charges. By measuring changes in electric charge flowing through the circuit, the sensor can detect changes in the light around it.

" More complex functions include rewriteable computer memory and even computer processing. These functions just require different combinations of simpler electronic elements. **"**

—Kendra

Flexible printed electronics do not perform as well as integrated circuits at certain tasks. A flexible printed computer processor, for example, cannot compete with an integrated circuit in terms of processing speed. Processing speed is an important measure of computing power.

" However, there are manufacturers that are taking traditional integrated circuits on silicon chips and making them razor thin, so they are also flexible. These integrated circuits can be bonded to a flexible material, connecting them to a flexible printed circuit. **"** —Kendra

The resulting combination is called **hybrid flexible electronics.** Hybrid flexible electronics combine some of the flexibility and cheapness of flexible printed electronics with the computing power of integrated circuits.

Down to Earth:

Ideas from space that could serve us on our planet.

Organizations such as NASA support "out of this world" research in part because it may lead to practical benefits.

❚❚ Space applications are actually kind of an oddball use for flexible electronics. They have many more potential uses here on the ground. **❚❚** —Kendra

In medicine, for example, doctors have been working to develop sensors and other electronic devices that can be implanted in the body. Rigid, traditional electronics are often poorly suited for such uses. They have trouble curving to follow the body's contours, and they cannot flex and bend along with the body's natural tissues.

Scientists have experimented with implanting flexible electronic sensors along the surface of the brain. Such sensors have been used to monitor brain activity in people who suffer from *seizures* (sudden attacks of disease). One day, a flexible printed implant may be able to sense a seizure before it happens and even deliver a shock that stops it.

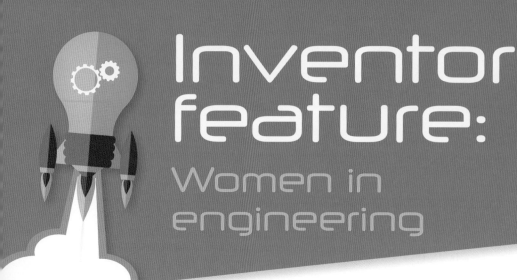

Inventor feature:
Women in engineering

Women were once excluded or discouraged from entering many fields of study, including science, technology, engineering, and mathematics (together called STEM). Much had changed by the time Kendra Short entered graduate school.

❚❚ There is definitely a sea change [great transformation] that comes with generations. I may have encountered some resistance among the older generation, but among the students in my class, both men and women, there was no question that we were equals. ❚❚ —Kendra

Still, there were relatively few women studying engineering at the time.

❝ There were five of us women at Princeton. We all knew each other, and we are all still friends today. ❞ —Kendra

Growing up, Short looked up to the pioneering astronaut Sally Ride, who became the first American woman to travel in space.

❝ She was a tremendous role model for many young girls. I don't know who that role model is today. But for my generation, Sally Ride was an inspiration. ❞ —Kendra

Kendra graduated from Princeton in 1989.

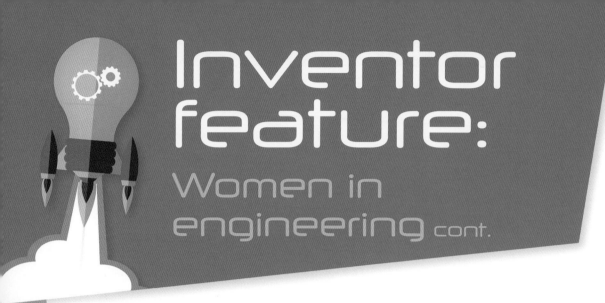

Role model: Sally Ride. Sally Kristen Ride (1951-2012) was a United States astronaut who became the first American woman to travel in space. In June 1983, she and astronauts Robert L. Crippen, John M. Fabian, Frederick H. Hauck, and Norman E. Thagard made a six-day flight on the space shuttle Challenger.

Ride was born on May 26, 1951, in Los Angeles. As a young girl, she developed a keen interest in math and science. She was also athletic, enjoying running, volleyball, and softball. Ride competed in tennis tournaments and was nationally ranked in college. Her mentor, the tennis great Billie Jean King, urged her to turn professional. However, Ride chose to become a scientist instead. She earned degrees in English, physics, and astrophysics from Stanford University. Armed with a doctorate degree in physics, she answered a newspaper ad from NASA seeking applicants for its astronaut corps. Ride was chosen from among more than 8,000 applicants for the program in 1978.

Ride's historic flight blasted off on June 18, 1983. She was not only the first American woman in space. At 32, she also became the youngest American to travel in space. Ride went back into space in 1984. She was scheduled for a third flight, but NASA suspended the shuttle program after the Challenger exploded on Jan. 28, 1986, killing all seven astronauts on board. Ride served on the commission that investigated the Challenger Disaster. She later served on the commission that investigated the loss of the space shuttle Columbia in 2003. In 1989, Ride joined the faculty of the University of California, San Diego, as a physics professor.

Ride was known as a private person who turned away from the spotlight. She seldom granted interviews and was reluctant to use her name for anything that would draw attention. But she was a passionate advocate for mathematics and science education. In 2001, she started the company Sally Ride Science to "make science and engineering cool again," especially for girls. She died on July 23, 2012.

Girls in engineering. In the early 1980's, only about 5 percent of engineers in the United States were women. With the help of role models like Sally Ride, that figure has risen to about 15 percent, but there is still a long way to go. Many programs and resources are available to help young women interested in engineering careers.

Engineer Girl (http://www.engineergirl.org/) This website offers advice for women interested in engineering careers and features profiles of women in engineering.

Sally Ride Science (https://sallyridescience.com) The company that Ride founded continues to offer programs for students and teachers in science, technology, engineering, and math.

Women at NASA (https://women.nasa.gov/) Female NASA employees describe their work at NASA and the paths they took to get into STEM. This site includes videos, essays, and links to STEM programs that will inspire future scientists and engineers.

Making a
prototype

Inventors often develop their ideas by building a prototype. A prototype is a working model of an invention. It may not look exactly like the finished product, but it demonstrates that the idea can work.

Short knew that her **probe** would require a power source, some **sensors** to gather data, and an antenna to transmit that data.

Her team found that many of these components already existed in flexible printed form. But nobody had yet combined them all to make a fully printable spacecraft.

❝ Our question was, can you get all the functions of a traditional spacecraft and print them to make a fully functional spacecraft that is basically like a sheet of paper? ❞
—Kendra

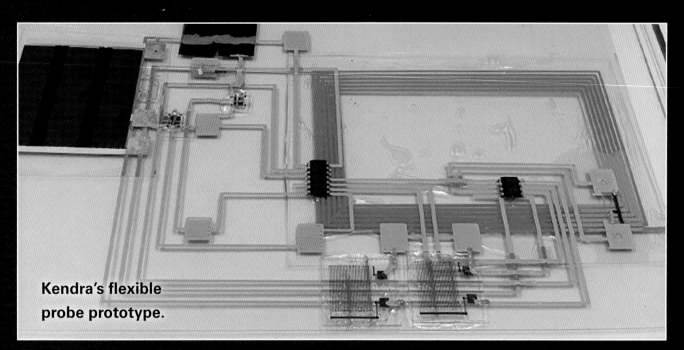
Kendra's flexible probe prototype.

Short's team spent several years researching and constructing their prototype. The finished version included two printed sensors, a light sensor and a temperature sensor. Printed **circuits** were also used to *multiplex* the data—that is, to distinguish and organize data from each sensor. A printed radio transmitter enabled the prototype to send the data to a laptop computer.

❝ So we ended up with a fully functional prototype spacecraft made out of printed electronics. ❞
—Kendra

Short's team also conducted environmental testing on the prototype. They exposed the craft to stressful conditions to see if it could survive spaceflight.

❝ We also did some mission studies, imagining how you might use something like this and what advantages it might give you. ❞ —Kendra

Down to Earth:

Ideas from space that could serve us on our planet.

Flexible printed sensors are also being developed for use in the food industry. Imagine, for example, a head of lettuce wrapped in a flexible printed sensor package. The package might monitor the lettuce's exposure to heat and light and record its entire packaging and transportation history. Such "smart" packaging could tell grocers and consumers when food is no longer fit for sale or consumption.

Inventor feature:
Other interests

Inventors do not spend all their time in labs. Kendra Short is married and is raising two children, a girl and a boy.

" Family is at the top of my list when I have free time. We enjoy camping, bike riding, and other outdoor activities. I also like to putter around in my garden, to cook, and to build stuff with my kids. " —Kendra

Growing up, Kendra was an avid soccer player.

Like her hero, Sally Ride, Short was also a college athlete.

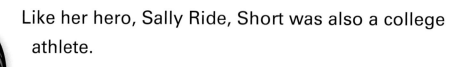

" I played soccer for many years, from the time I was about five years old through college. My senior year, my roommate and I were the captains of our college team. " —Kendra

Kendra with her husband Wesley, son Aidan, and daughter Amelia at Crater Lake (above, left), Petrified Forest (above, right), and the Grand Canyon (left).

Inventor feature:
Contests

❚❚ There are so many hands-on building opportunities for kids today that did not exist when I was growing up. The LEGO® robotic programs in schools today make me wish I were a kid again. Instead, I am the adult advisor— but I still get to play with the toys! ❚❚ —Kendra

Many schools and other institutions offer LEGO-based robotics contests for young people. Teams of contestants must use LEGO bricks and LEGO Mindstorms robotics to solve engineering challenges based on real-world problems.

One of the largest such competitions, the FIRST LEGO League, began as a partnership between the LEGO Group and the nonprofit educational organization FIRST, the initial letters of For Inspiration and Recognition of Science and Technology. More information on this and other challenges is available at www.firstinspires.org.

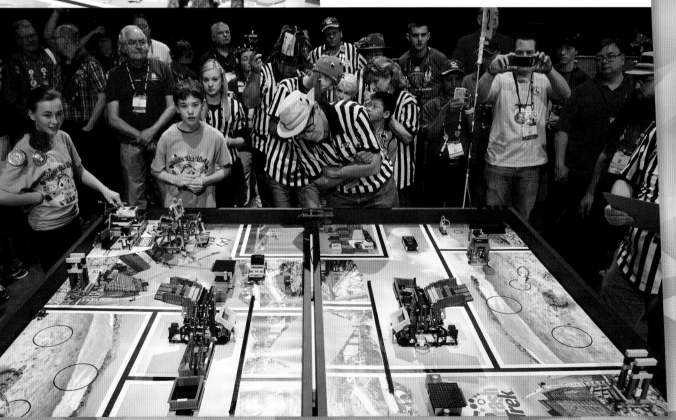

Covering Mars

Kendra Short's papery **probe,** with perhaps a handful of basic **sensors,** may seem pretty simple compared to the specially built **rovers** that have explored Mars. But unlike those fragile rovers, Short's lightweight and flexible craft would not have to be coddled and cradled to the surface by airbags, **retrorockets,** and sky cranes.

The cheap, easy-to-make craft can be printed by the thousands and softly dropped on to the Martian surface.

❝ They would lie on the surface of Mars, forming an environmental sensor network. Each probe could sense temperature, air pressure, and wind speed at a particular point. By combining data from all the probes, you could develop a detailed computer model of the Martian atmosphere. ❞ —Kendra

Because there could be many probes, it would be possible to gather information over a much larger area than with a few traditional landers. And if a few probes fail, there are still thousands of others gathering information.

❝ Think of the Beagle 2 lander. When one part failed, a solar panel, it led to the failure of the entire mission. ❞ —Kendra

❚❚ Imagine printing up a whole bunch of these spacecraft, like little sheets of paper, and packing them in an **aeroshell.** You could release them into the atmosphere and let them flutter down to the surface, like confetti. **❚❚** —Kendra

Kendra Short and her team

Kendra Short and Dr. David Van Buren, with whom she devised the idea for confetti probes.

Glossary

aeroshell (AIR oh SHELH) covering that protects a spacecraft as it enters the atmosphere of an object in space.

circuit (SUR kiht) a path or track for carrying electric charges. Circuits serve as the basic units of electronic devices.

conventional circuit (kuhn VEHN shuh nuhl SUR kiht) a circuit made of conductive material mounted on a flat, rigid board.

electric signal (ih LEHK trihk SIHG nuhl) a flow of electricity that has been changed to carry information.

flexible printed electronics (FLEHK suh buhl PRIHN tihd il LEHK TRON ihkz) the use of circuits printed onto a thin, flexible material.

hybrid flexible electronics (HY brihd FLEHK suh buhl il LEHK TRON ihkz) the combination of flexible printed electronics with thin, flexible integrated circuits.

integrated circuit (IHN tuh GRAY tihd SUR kiht) a circuit etched, or carved, into a piece of semiconductor material, such as silicon; a computer chip.

lander (LAN duhr) a spacecraft designed to land on a planet or other solid surface.

mechanical engineer (muh KAN uh kuhl EHN juh NIHR) an engineer—an expert in planning and building things—who studies what solid and liquid things do and what they do when they are parts of bigger things.

orbit (AWR biht) circling another body in space.

orbiter (AWR biht uhr) a spacecraft designed to orbit a planet or other object in space.

probe (prohb) a robotic spacecraft sent to explore a distant object.

retrorockets (REHT roh ROK iht) reverse-firing rockets used to slow and steer spacecraft.

rover (ROH vuhr) a lander designed to move about for surface exploration.

sensor (SEHN suhr) a device that detects heat, light, or some other phenomenon, producing an electric signal.

For further information

Want to know more about Mars?

Berger, Melvin and Mary Kay Carson. *Discovering Mars: The Amazing Story of the Red Planet.* Scholastic, 2015.

Want to know more about the importance of water?

Stewart, Melissa. *National Geographic Readers: Water.* National Geographic Children's Books, 2014.

Want to create your own circuits to make new inventions?

Graves, Colleen and Aaron Graves. *The Big Book of Makerspace Projects: Inspiring Makers to Experiment, Create, and Learn.* McGraw-Hill Education TAB, 2016.

Think like an inventor

Imagine making an article of clothing using flexible printed electronics. The electronics might include various **sensors,** display screens, or any other device you can think of. What features and functions would you include in your design?

Index

Acknowledgments

Cover	WORLD BOOK illustration by Francis Lea (NASA/JPL/Cornell)
4-5	NASA/JPL-Caltech
6-7	© Shutterstock
8-9	WORLD BOOK illustration by Rob Wood; NASA/JPL/USGS
10-11	NASA/JPL-Caltech/Univ. of Arizona; NASA/JPL-Caltech/University of Arizona/Texas A&M University
12-13	NASA/JPL
14-15	NASA
18-19	NASA/JPL/University of Arizona; ESA
21	NASA/JPL-Caltech
22-23	WORLD BOOK illustration by Francis Lea (NASA)
25	© Shutterstock
27	© Shawn Hempel, Shutterstock
31	Kendra Short
33	NASA
35	Texas A&M University (licensed under CC BY 2.0)
36-37	Kendra Short
38-39	Kendra Short
40-41	© Adriana Groisman, FIRST; © Dan Donovan, FIRST
42-43	WORLD BOOK illustration by Francis Lea (NASA/JPL/Cornell)
44	Kendra Short